STONES:
SILENT WITNESS TO THE CULTURAL DIVERSITY OF INDIA

STONES:
SILENT WITNESS TO THE CULTURAL DIVERSITY OF INDIA

Jayanta Guha
and
Ganpat Roonwal

Kaveri Books
New Delhi-110002

First Published in 2014

ISBN 978-81-7479-143-6

Published by

Kaveri Books

4832/24, Ansari Road

New Delhi - 110 002 (India)

Tel.: 011-2328 8140, 2324 5799

E-mail: kaveribooks@vsnl.com,

kaveribooks@gmail.com

Website: www.kaveribooks.com

Laser Typesetting by : Deep Graphics, Delhi

PRINTED IN INDIA

Contents

Preface

The idea for this book emanated from a photographic exhibition by the first author portraying "Stones : a silent witness to the cultural diversity of India" held in 2004. The idea was not to identify the stones that made up the various monuments heralding the heritage of India's history but an attempt to decipher how the diversity of craftsmen with diverse cultural background left their imprint. Of course it is not only the craftsmen but also the cultural background of those who commissioned these monuments left a profound mark how the stones were used. These stones withstood the test of time remaining as silent observers of this cultural diversity.

An exhibition, with limited space needs to be focussed on the theme although the stones themselves vary in nature and provenance. A book, however, permits to digress and helps to complete the picture and gives an opportunity to talk about the geological evolution of India and the birth of these rocks which form the cornerstone of all the monuments. This is where the importance of the second author comes in. As an eminent geologist with varied interests and a number of books to his credit, Professor Ganpat Roonwal is ably suited to do justice combining his knowledge of the geology of India to bring to life the 'silent witnesses' which are the rocks.

Readers should not make a mistake, this is not an exhaustive description, neither of the monuments nor of all the type of rocks but essentially to let the readers imaginations delve into the cultural background of the people who commissioned these monuments and the craftsmen who erected them.

The authors hope that the readers will also note that the identification of cultural diversity of these monuments also points to an intercultural spirit that existed throughout the history of the Indian civilization and the stones speak for themselves. Rabindranath Tagore in his famous poem "Bharot Tirtha" extolled the great magnanimity of the habitants of India welcoming to her shores people of all walks of life, colour and creed from the world. These transformed stones bear witness to this magnanimity.

List of Figures

1

Stones

Stones have recorded the history of civilisation and have been silent observers of history in the making. This passion with stones goes back to the cave paintings where it acted as a medium to portray the imagination of people and even to leave messages for us to decipher. The texture, the beauty and the resilience of stones made it a cherished item whenever one thought of building a monument, a fortification, an abode or an object of art. In most cases the source of the rocks were local but for others, especially the semi-precious stones, the designers and their masters never hesitated to procure them from distant lands, a proof of links and trade routes existing between far flung territories from time immemorial. From the resplendent Taj Mahal made of marble to the banded metamorphic rocks used for the Sun temple of Konarak and the sandstone becoming golden with the rays of the rising and setting sun in Jaisalmer also illustrates the knowledge regarding this natural material that existed prior to modern day geology and mineralogy. The thousands and thousand man-hours required to cut, shape and build, right from the excavations of these rocks underline the onset of regional and local development and economy that prevailed in ancient times. Like everywhere, stones were shaped and reshaped by multitude of craftsmen, working under the influence of different cultures both indigenous and imported. This left a stamp of each culture through utilisation of rocks, whereby the rocks remained a silent observer of history that it helped to portray.

This book is just a glimpse of the equation between how men perceived stones through times and is certainly not a travel guide to monuments. Many important monuments have not been covered. The idea has been to throw some light between inanimate structures, rocks and minerals, and its interaction with human beings and how they have been chosen and shaped according to the cultural heritage and openness of the builder. However, to do this, it is important to look back and discover how the stones came about, in short the evolution of India through the geological ages.

Stones and the History of Man

Much less direct evidence has come forth from the stones and rocks about the history of Early Man. The mute sediments and early man's preserved stone-tool as we see in the accompanying illustrations (Fig.1) tell us all about him. He used to live close to rivers or lakes, along edge of the forest, on higher ground beyond the reach of the flood. He also inhabited the caves, he manufactured his tools from the stones. He would often drag his prey to his abode for an enjoyable feast.

The Early Man was very adventurous. Without much equipment and any means of transport he roved over hills and plains, over the glaciers and gravel, in rain or storm, carrying his little kit, the stone tools which were all only belongings. This pioneer explorer wandered for years and years, even then his journey never came to an end.

The Early Stone Age Man manufactured crude stone axes and stone hammers. Later he used a wooden mallet for fine pieces of work. He had some contact with the early Stone age man of South Africa. During this time the Early Stone Age Man in the North used

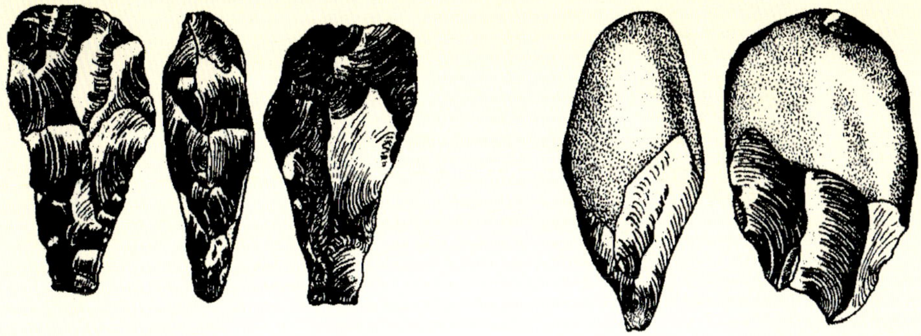

Stone hand axe
(Showing different views)

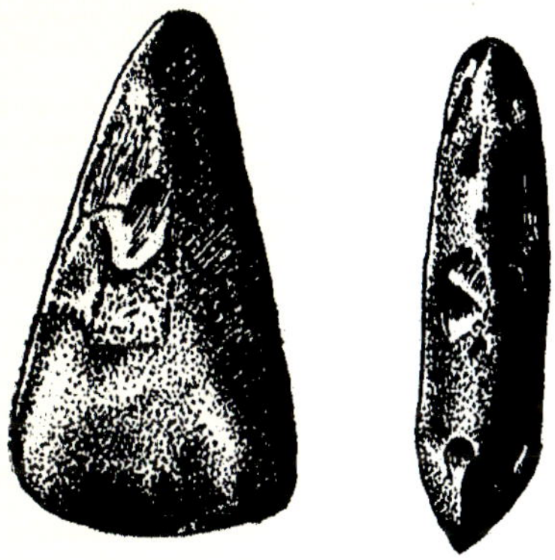

Polished stone axe
(Showing different views)

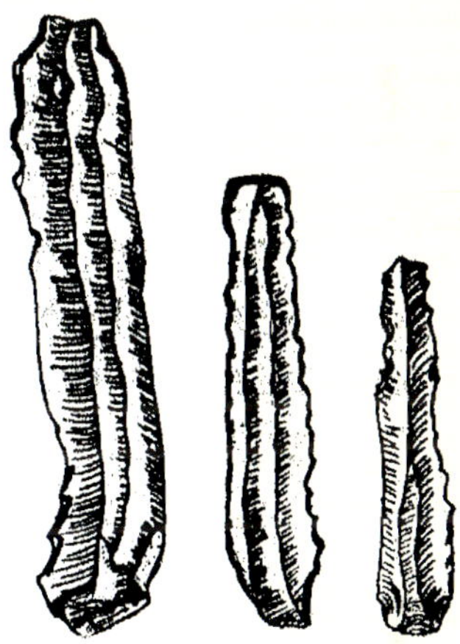

Stone blade
(Showing different views)

Fig.1: Tools used by the Early Man

to a large extent flake tools, choppers and scrapers made from pebbles. It is believed that the hand axes used by the Early Stone Age Man in the North were probably gifted to them by those in the South. These cultures existed during the second and third severe cold waves, about 450,000 and 200,000 years ago respectively.

About 10,000 years ago at the end of the last severe cold waves, the early Indians had developed small sized stone tools. This was the Mesolithic Age. These small stone tools called the microliths were mounted together on a handle of wood to form a cutting edge. This cultural change came because the gigantic animals like the mammoth rhinoceros and bison had disappeared. There were now deer, pig and other small animals. The microliths were also used by these men for cutting their way through the forest. They had established contact with Mediterranean folk and with Negroid races that lived there.

After the Mesolithic Age, the New Stone Age began. The New Stone Age man polished his stone tools and made utensils from clay. He was the most highly advanced of the Stone Age man. Though fire has been known earlier he made a different use of both fire and forest. He felled the forests and practiced agriculture. He sowed the first seeds of our civilization. He cultivated rice, and other food grain.

About 4,000 to 5,000 years ago a great civilization developed in Sind, Punjab, Western Uttar Pradesh, Rajasthan, Kutch and Gujarat. People used rice, wheat and barley. They made utensil from clay as well as from copper. Their hearth and homes were built of bricks. The period of floods in the rivers destroyed this civilization. This culture was of a highly advanced type. Women wore ornaments and children used to play with several kinds of clay toys. They used to bury their dead and keep pots and stone tools along with the dead body.

The climate was dry during the Indus-valley civilization, or the Harappan civilization. This great civilization ended about 1750 B.C. Thereafter several less developed copper using cultures emerged in various parts of India. Iron began to be used in India about 3,000 years by people who are believed to be the Aryans.

The forests were felled to provide them fuels for cooking, for baking bricks and for smelting copper, and to provide land for cultivation. The continuous cutting of forests changed the once forested tracts into desert. This is how Rajasthan became a desert.

This is in short what rocks tell us about the history of Man in India. In the beginning Man was completely depended upon Nature for several thousand years. He lived like any wild animal. Later, he laid foundation of modern society and agriculture. From, stone that meant so much to him, he now shifted to metals. First to copper and then to iron, but stones continue to play an important part in his life.

Sometime during the Metallic Age, Man discovered the art of writing and began to write his own history. This story written in stones is a silent witness to evolving culture and diversity of India. It speaks of both the mind and skill and craftsmanship. Let us learn from this story.

2

The Origin of the Earth and Birth of India

The earliest histories of the earth are so worn out that its pages have become fragile, torn and fragmentary. They are today so much obliterated and spoiled that it is a challenge to decipher history of the Earth from the few evidences that still exist. This is one reason why the origin of the earth is still a mystery in spite of several scientific tools that are available today to unravel them. It is generally accepted that the earth originated from the sun. To start it was burning white hot and was possibly made up of gases. It cooled down rapidly to a liquid state and finally became solid. It is also clear that at birth, the earth was smaller in size than what it is today. Perhaps the climate was very hot and tropical when earth curst began to form by cooling from gases to molten matter to become solid. As the temperature fell, steam condensed into water and filled depressions making the seas. Thus the hardened crust formed the land, and

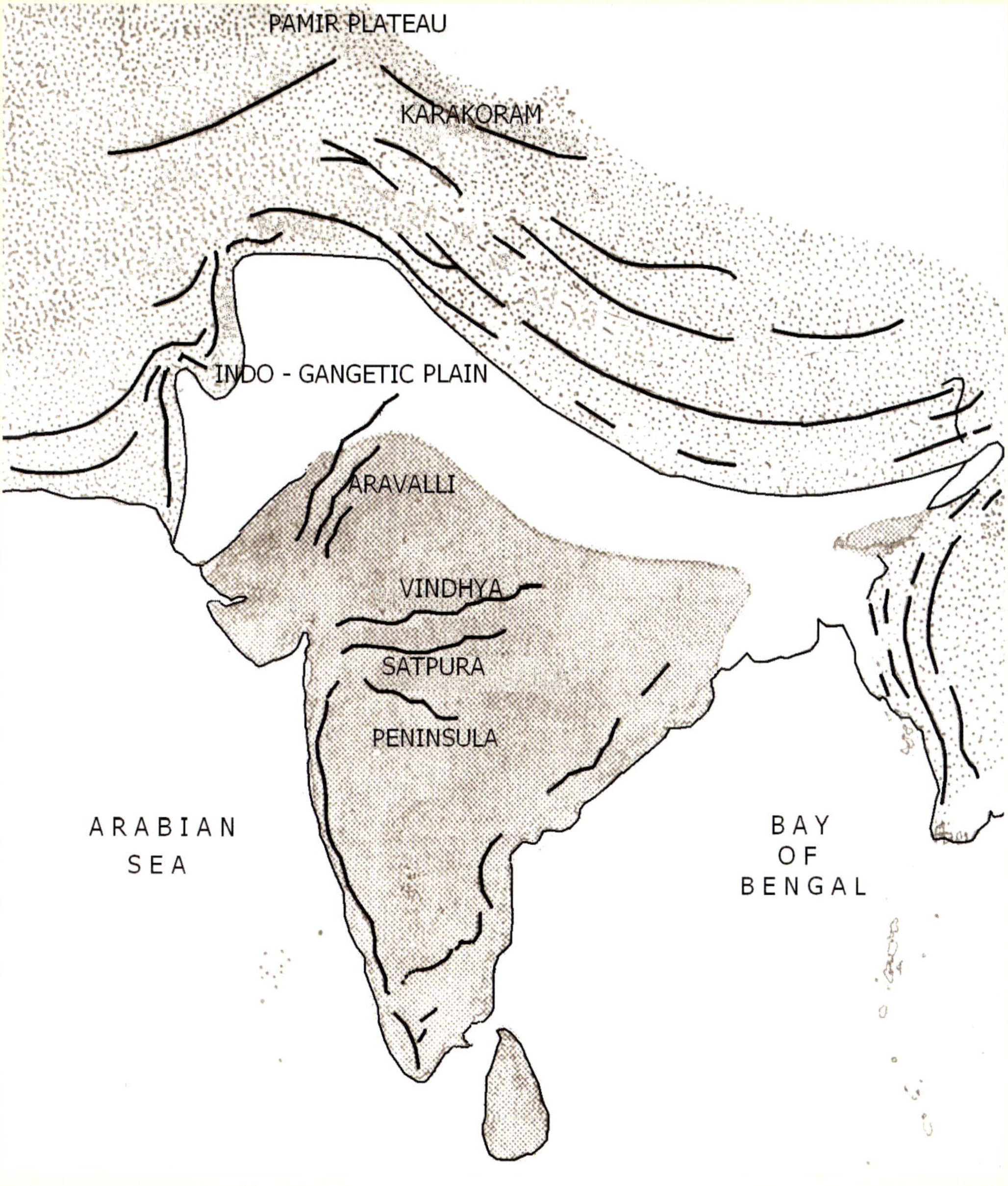

Fig.2: The birth of India

filled depression the first seas on the earth. When first formed the seas were of fresh water which gradually became salty.

The Birth of India

To start with when the earth came into the shape of a planet, its existence was different. India and other continents were without their present shape or form. In the early stages of development, there were neither mountains nor oceans. The plains and plateau familiar to us today did not exist at that time. Then India had quite a different shape from what use see today (Fig. 2).

A large part of the Indian Peninsula and Central India together with Sri Lanka (Ceylon) and present day Myanmar (Burma) had, however, been formed.

As time passed, the newly formed India was affected by some violent and destructive forces such as earthquake and the erosion of rocks. Thus, their shape and structure were changed. Such earth movement gave rise to the formation of the Aravalli mountain in the now Indian Peninsula. When these forces died out, the land began to sink forming depressions which were gradually filled by thick sediments. Volcanoes existed in certain parts of young India. There was also a sea in the Central India. The floor of this sea rose to form the Vindhyachal mountain (Satpura ranges). Some volcanoes existed in Rajasthan also, but there are none today. During this time there was little life on the earth.

The Dark Age

The close of this early period was followed by a Dark Age which lasted about 300 million years. We call it Dark Age because the rocks of this period are missing in most of India, but those present in north India was under a sea. There was no Himalaya, in its place there was a sea – the Sea of Tethys. This sea was part of the ancient Mediterranean ocean (Fig.3). It encircled almost the whole of Earth dividing the entire landmass into northern and the southern hemisphere divided by the Tethys Sea. During this Dark Age some plants looking like ferns grew in the north-west (Fig. 4). Scores of animals lived in the Tethys Sea. The sea animals were of a very primitive type. There were trilobites, brachiopods, sponges and corals. Several of the animals that lived than are not found today.

The Gondwanaland

The young India had already been separated from the mother earth by the Tethys Sea. Now, it lay far south in the region of the India Ocean of today. Along side with it were East Africa and Madagascar with Australia forming the eastern or southern part of it. To the extreme west, India extended beyond South America which was then joined to South Africa. The southern part of this landmass was Antarctica. This super continent landmass with Tethys Sea extending towards the north has been named as Gondwanaland. The name Gondwana has been taken from the Kingdom of Gonds – a primitive tribe in Madhya Pradesh of today's India. Towards the north of Gondwanaland beyond the Tethys sea there lay another super continent the Angaraland, as shown in Fig.3.

For about 70 million years Gondwanaland continued as described above. About 110 to 120 million years ago the volcanic eruptions, earth movements and marine floods began to break up this landmass. Australia moved away first. The Bay of Bengal assumed its present shape. South America broke away from this landmass more or less at this time. India too was sliced off but did not move to its present position in the North until about 30 million years later. The eastern coast of India was carved out about 150 million years ago.

Some earth scientists and physicists believe that instead of being a continuous land mass, Gondwanaland was more a sort of an archipelago with several land bridges connecting India, Africa, America and Australia. Fig.3 shows two arms of the sea extending inland. These arms of the sea have remained here for millions of years. The western arm covered the present Coromandal coast and the Narmada valley and the eastern arm covered Assam and parts of the Indo-Gangetic plain. India then was a big volcanic plateau. Hot burning lavas flooded hundreds of thousand of kilometers from coast to coast.

During the early history of Gondwanaland, there were glaciers on the Aravallis and Vindhhyans, from there, the ice sheets spread to the west Punjab and Kashmir in the west and, to the eastern India in the east. The Tethys Sea extended into western Rajasthan, Sind and parts of western Punjab. The climate was ice cold. When it began to warm up, dense forest of fern – like seed plants called Gangomopteris and Glossopteris together with several other plants were formed. Swamps inhabited by ganoid fish and reptiles were very common. It was during this period that thick deposits of coal were formed.

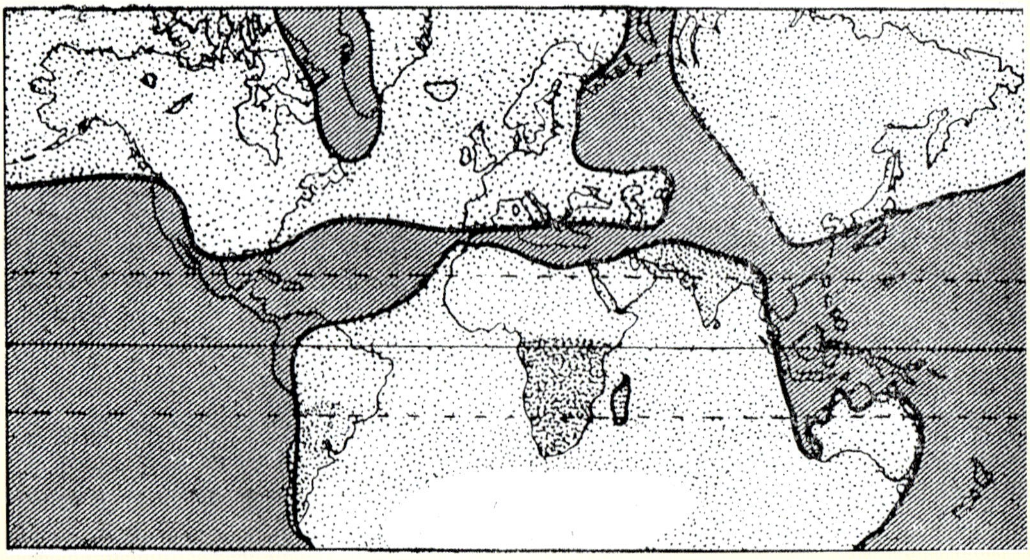

Fig.3: The Gondwana Super Continent as visualised, and the present days continents

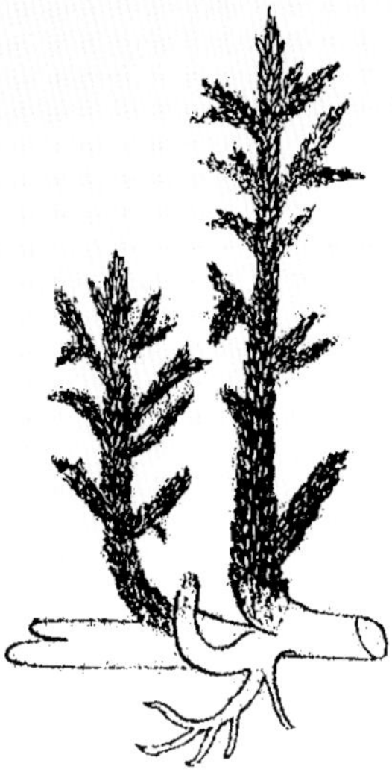

A fossil early land plant

A seed fern

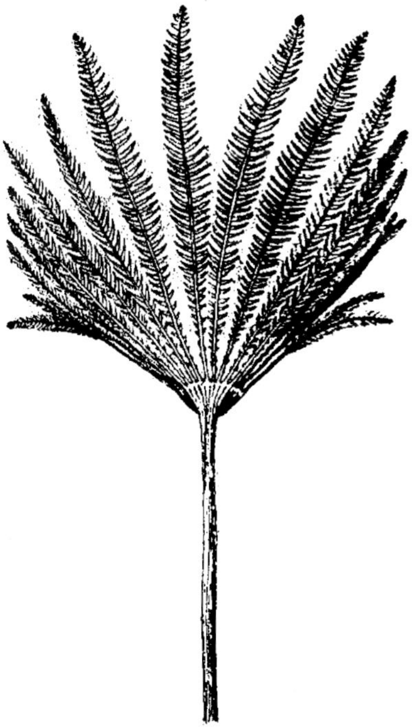

A fossil fern

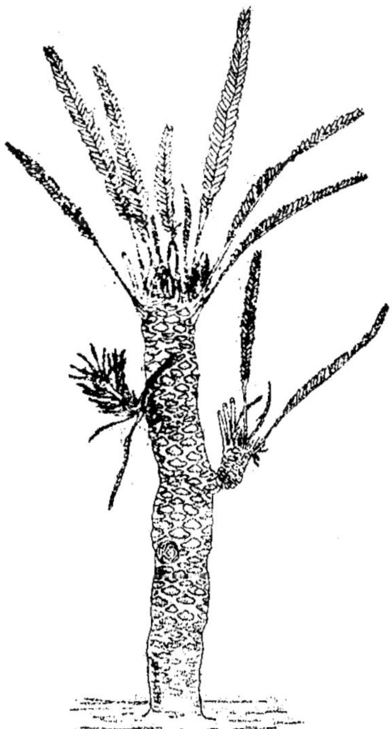

A cycad-lik fossil tree

Fig.4: Different type of Plants through the ages

The warm and moist climate became dry about 180 million years ago. Now there were new types of forests. There were huge reptile and fish which could live on land and water. This was the age of Dinosaurs (Fig.5).

About 30 million years later, the climate because warm and moist again, and the ancestors of the modern forest trees came into existence at this time. The forests consisted of plants such as conifers and cycades and fern (Fig.4)

The sea animals were now more advanced than those which lived previously, amongst them the cephalopods and the lamellibranchs were very common. Birds appeared for the first time. Towards the close of this golden period the plants which produced flowers came into existence.

The Shaping of Modern India

About 60 million years ago, India took its present shape and form. It broke away from the landmass of Gondwanaland. Nature celebrated it with the rip and roar of volcanic eruptions. Lava covered almost half a million square kilometer of land (the present day Deccan Traps as they are called). Violent earthquakes broke Gondwanaland into fragments which moved in different directions. The bottom of the Tethys Sea began an upward movement. It went over and above the sea level forming the Himalayas. A long and narrow trough was formed between the Himalayas and the Peninsula. This trough was later filled up with sediments and formed the modern Indo-Gangetic plain. In the north western part of India the last remains of the Tethys Sea disappeared gradually.

The rivers, as we can imagine, must have all flowed into the Tethys Sea in the north and north west. Now they changed their direction of flow. The Indo-Gangetic plain was drained by a mighty river called the Indo–Brahma. Fig.6 shows that the Indo-Brahma discharged its waters into the Arabian Sea. With the rise of north-western India, the Indo-Brahma was also now split up into the present Indus (Sind) river and the

Fig.5: Geological time-table and evolution of life

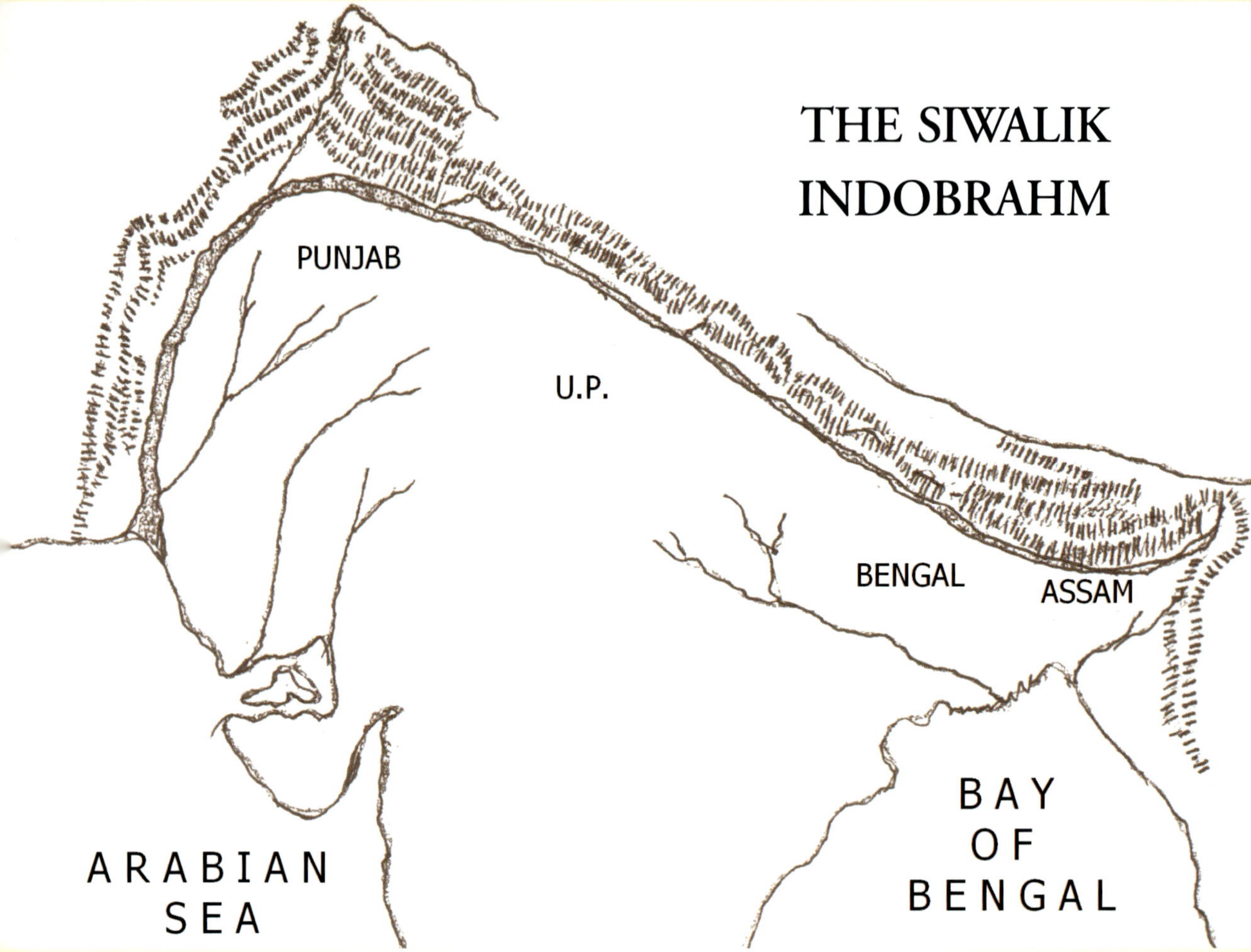

Fig.6: The Origin of River System

Brahmaputra. Since than the Brahmaputra has been discharging its waters into the Bay of Bengal.

The Tethys Sea has disappeared and an ocean surrounded the Peninsula. The direction of the winds has also changed. There were snow deposits on the peaks of the Himalayas.

Rain forests existed in several parts of India, even in Rajasthan which is a desert today. A large number of animals like rhinoceros, giraffes, horses, snake, apes, and elephants lived in these forests. Crocodiles swarmed in the water.

Nature in the meanwhile was busy building up a chain of mountain in the north, the minor hill ranges elsewhere. An ocean known to us as the Indian Ocean was made. We had also at this time the beginnings of our modern rivers. (Fig.7)

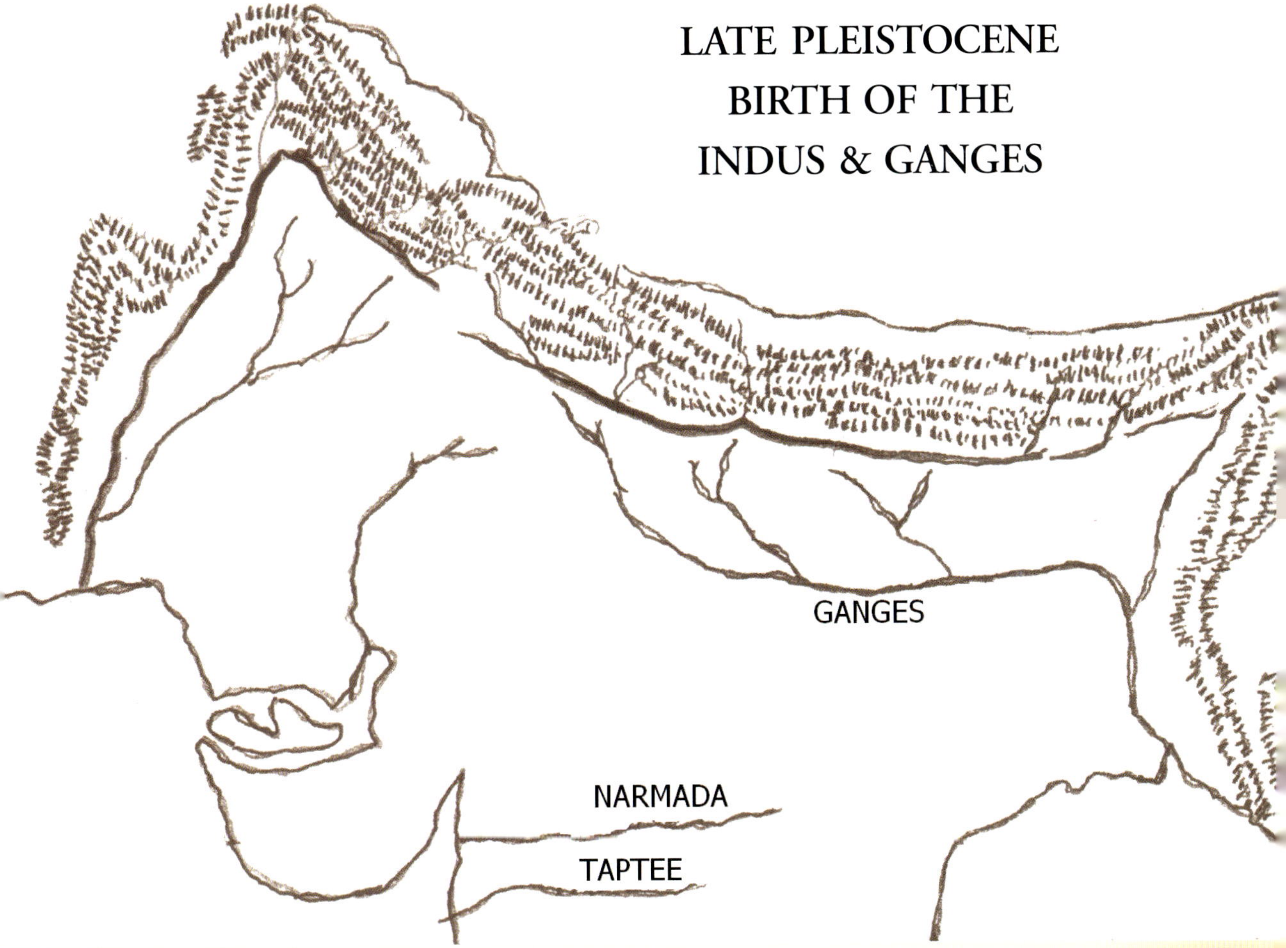

Fig.7: The Indus-Ganga river system in Late Pleistocene time

As mentioned earlier, the Indo-Gangetic plain was formed in this period. The finishing touches to the geography of modern India were given by nature, in this period of the last one million years.

The Quaternary or the great Ice Age was the most recent geological period of time. This was marked by great earthquakes, and the Himalaya attained their present height then. The valleys at high altitude were covered with glaciers. The climate became ice-cold as the glaciers moved down to the foothills. A severe cold wave gripped north India for thousands of years. The Indian peninsula experienced heavy rain. The glaciers began to melt, recede, and hence the climate became warmth. The water released from the glaciers flooded the stream, the rising streams moved with great speed, cut through the valleys and made huge gorges. A great load of detritus was deposited on the eroded surfaces of the valleys. The water level of the ocean rose and flooded the coastal areas and Bengal was flooded by the sea when the glaciers melted.

From the rocks we know that there had been four such major server cold waves in the north India. Each was followed by a warmer phase. The alternation of the cold and warm periods made several raised or terraced steps along the banks of rivers.

The last major cold wave ended about 10,000 years ago. The repeated periods of severe cold waves destroyed a vast population of animals and plants that had lived here before. This drove animals from the neighbouring countries into India. Of the several kinds of elephants that had dwelt in our forests, only one kind, the modern elephant, has survived. The ape-like animals changed into man during this great Ice-age. It is therefore, also called the Age of Man. The early man was not very different from the other animals in his mode of living. He used to hunt animals and gather food.

Then finally modern India emerged as we see it today, during hundreds of millions years, slowly and steadily millimeter by millimeter. Nature created plain, hills, oceans, and plants and animals of various kinds. The history of making of India is the history of its origin. The rise of the mountain, and their later erosion, followed. Thus the distribution and readjustment of the sea, and land continued to give panorama of the evolution of plants and animal life. Several animals and plants either vanished or underwent new forms, until a new force appeared in the form of Man who gradually began to subdue the nature around him.

3

Rocks and Their Types

Most of us look upon a rock as a hard and stony substance. You may want to know how such a soft thing as mud is also a rock. For an earth scientist a rock can be soft as well as hard. Therefore, sand and pebble are also rocks.

Mud as we know is formed in water. It may be in a lake or in sea. Rivers carry huge loads of mud, sand and pebbles into the sea. Pebbles being heavy settle down at the bottom first and then they make a layer. Sand forms a layer over the layer of pebbles, and mud over that of sand. Therefore, rocks made under water are made up of layers. As the layers are piled up, a lake or sea may be filled up and disappear. When dry these softer rocks become hard. All such rocks which are made under water are called sedimentary rocks.

On drying up, mud becomes shale, and sand becomes sandstones. A mixture of sand, mud and pebbles makes conglomerate. Some shale and sandstone are gray, some are pink or red, and some are yellow in colour. Shale may also have different colour, even shale may be in black colour. The famous Red Fort in Delhi is made up of red sandstone. Several other modern and ancient buildings in Delhi, Agra and Rajasthan, Gujarat are built of red and whitish sandstone.

It is easy to tell one kind of rock from the other. We can feel the grain of sand in sandstone. Moist on a piece of shale and it smells like mud. A limestone bubbles when a drop of hydrochloric acid is put on it.

Plants and animals which live in lakes and seas also help in making of rock. When they die, the harder part of their body combines to make rocks. Corals and shell are made up of lime. When they die, their dead bodies make limestone.

We are familiar with the coal that we burn in kitchen, as well as in power generation. It was made under water from plants that lived on earth several million years ago (during the lower Gondwana times). But please note that not all coal is black. Coal can be brown – then it is called Lignite or Brown coal. Thick deposits or lignite occur in south of Chennai (Madras) at Neyveli, Rajasthan (at Palana in Bikaner district and in Nagaur district), and in Kashmir.

Let us remember that change is the law of Nature. So rocks also change. The change may be brought about by the pressure of the layer on top, or by the heat from within the earth. A brown coal may change to black coal, shale may change to slate, like shale, slate also smell like clay when wet. Sandstone may change into quartzite. It is much harder than sandstone. Limestone may become marble. The famous Taj Mahal at Agra and Victoria Memorial in Kolkata (Calcutta) are made of white marble. When rocks change, they are called metamorphic rocks.

There are certain other kinds of rocks. They are made in a different way. Most of us know what a volcano is. When it erupts, hot molten lava comes out of it. Lava is rock in a molten state. Rocks at great depths from the surface of the earth are not solid, but are in molten state. Sometimes steam or other gases may push out the hot molten and liquid material from below the surface (Hydrothermal emanations). The weight of the rock layers (sequence) above may also squeeze it out from within the earth. When so pushed out, the hot molten lava spreads in form of a flood. It cools down to form a rock called basalt. Daccan basalts is an example of this. If the lava does not come out but cools inside a magma, it cool slowly inside the earth and form rocks called plutonic; it makes crystalline rocks like gabbro, granite. Granites are either white, red, gray, and gabbro dark (black). Several temples in southern parts of India are made from granite, gabbro and a special rock called Charnockite which can vary in colour from white to black.

Igneous rocks also change–granite changes into gneiss which has small streaks or bands. They are extensively used as building stones.

Stones Depict the Past

A sand grain or a pebble is not just a particle of dead matter. It represents the story of Nature, part of the history of the earth. Rocks made up of such particles are then pages of this history. Several kinds of sedimentary layers lying one upon the other made up the pages and chapters of this Nature's book.

A sedimentary rock indicates presence by a river, lake or sea. A limestone or a rock salt tells us about the sea. Sometimes on breaking a piece of rock we find the marks of animals, or of a leaf (Fig.4). These are the impressions of dead animals or plants which once lived in latter or accidently fell into it, or even carried into it. These are called fossils. These fossils tell us if it was a sea or a fresh water lake in which the rock was made. Some buildings in Jaisalmer are made up of such fossil bearing limestone, and are called ornamental stones.

They tell us also the past climate (see Gondwana system for an example). A piece of coal tells up of the swamps and forests in the ages past. A sand, gravel, and conglomerate carried out by rivers today, as in the past tell us of the fast moving rivers or stream, and even floods.

Let us look as the thick sand deposits of Rajasthan, or Thar Desert where the climate is dry. A dust storm blows the sand particles from one place to another. When sand particles settles down they don't make layers. Like the sedimentary rocks we have seen being deposited in water. They deposit in different shapes – sand dunes of various shapes infact depict the strength and direction of wind. But while blowing, the sand particles (mainly quartz, hardness 7), scratch and even polish the existing rocks in the region. So we find polished surface of granites, and various designs such as balance rock.

Layers of rocks in lakes or swamps are usually laid parallel to one another. There could be layer of mud, clays, alternating with sand, or gravel, or limestone, or even coal. The deposition pattern of them is preserved in them. One can see the current beddings; ripple marks, etc in them. The Red Fort in Delhi, and the Umaid Bhawan Palace in Jodhpur, one can see beautiful current bedding pattern in the sandstones. So the parallel layers and by side way pressure act compressed to generate fold pattern. This is beautifully seen in Chittorgarh where the limestones show different pattern of such folds. Fig. 8A and 8B: Show Sandstone mining and cutting of slabs in Jodhpur area.

The igneous rock tell one of the temperature condition of the past. During Cretaceous period, there were several volcanoes in the Central India (120 to 125 million years ago). The time of lava flows can be measured by examining their layering.

Igneous rocks tell us the past condition of high temperature and pressure. When the sedimentary rock change into metamorphic rock or come in contact with large body of an igneous rock, such as a granite batholiths, its original pattern, record and style changes.

They are sometimes completely destroyed. But modern methods have been able to decipher this. The story of mankind is indeed as exciting as of the formation of rocks.

Fig.8A: Cutting of slabs of Sandstone in a quarry near Jodhpur

Fig.8B: Mining of Sandstone Slabs

4

Rock System of India

All minerals and mineral products are derived from rocks forming the crust of the earth. The accompanying table (Table 1) gives the sequence in chronological order of the various rock systems of India formed in the successive geological ages.

Geologically, India is divided into three component units (a), the triangular peninsular landmass of the Deccan. (b) the high chain of the Himalaya and the related mountain bordering the Peninsula to the west, north and east, and (c) the great plain of India lying between these two units – the Indo-Gangetic plain, stretching from Punjab to Assam. (Fig. 2)

The divergent physical features of these segments are clearly related to their geological history and structure. The Peninsula of India is one of the oldest and most stable blocks of the earth; the Himalaya are amongst the youngest mountain system of the world, and the Indo-Gangetic plain are yet of subsequent growth.

Archaean System

The rocks belonging to this system are the most ancient rocks forming the earth's crust – they are the gneisses, schists and granites along with extremely metamorphosed sedimentary rocks, which lie at the base of rock systems belonging to all the subsequent geological ages. Metamorphism is the sum total of changes which rock undergo when subjected to sub-terranean heat and pressure.

The Archaean rocks of India cover a large areas of the Deccan and parts of Ranchi plateau (Jharkhand state), Madhya Pradesh, Odisha, and Rajasthan, extending to northern Gujarat, as well as some parts of the central ranges of the high Himalaya,

Table 1: Geological formations of India

Era	Geological System (Standard)	Age in million year	Himalaya	Peninsula
Quaternary	Recent Pleistocene	1	Recent river deposit, Loess, Indo-Gangetic alluvium, glacial deposit	Newer alluvia, desert deposits older alluvia, laterite
Tertiary	Pliocene Miocene Eocene	10 29 70	Upper Siwalik Tertiaries of the outer Himalayas Lower Siwalik Subathu beds, Nummulitic limestones	Cuddalore sandstone Assam and Coastal deposits Deccan Traps
Secondary	Cretaceous Jurassic Triassic	139 185 235	Cretaceous of Kashmir and Spiti Bagh beds, Lameta beds Jurassic of Kashmir Spiti (Tal Series), Upper Gondwana,, Jurassic of Kutch Triassic of Kashmir, and Spiti (Krol series)	Trichinopoly and Assam Cretaceous Panchet and Mahadev Series
Primary	Permian Carboniferous Devonian Silurian Cambrian	246 280 320 360 500	Productus beds, Zewan Series, Carboniferous of Spiti and Kashmir. Muth series of Spiti, Kashmir, Silurian system of Spiti, Kashmir Haimanta system of Spiti, Kashmir	Lower Gondwana - - -
Archaean	Algonkian Archaeozoic	3500	Dogra, Simla, Daling series Gneisses and schists	Cuddapah and Vindhyan System Aravalli group Dharwar group gneisses

Gilgit, Ladakh, Garhwal, Kumaon, extending through Nepal to east in Assam – the Maghalaya Plateau. They belong to two phases – (a) igneous, gneisses and schists (Archaean system proper) and the highly metamorphosed primitive sediments which have been metamorphosed into gneisses and schists, quartzites, marbles etc. (the Dharwar group). The Dharwar group is economically of great importance, as it contain many of the principal ore – deposits and industrially useful minerals.

Cuddapah System

After a long interval of time during which the Archaean rocks were uplifted into mountain chains and other features resulting from earth movements, followed by an era of erosion and sedimentation, this system of rocks was laid down on the old denuded surface of the Peninsula. This is known as the Cuddapah system. They consist of slates, quartzite and limestones with jaspers. They have undergone far less folding and metamorphism than the strata of the Archaean system, and are hence only partly metamorphosed. These rocks are unfossiliferrous, though it is probable that primitive life had originated on the planet in this age. Rocks of this system are found in Cuddapah district of Andhra Pradesh, and Chhattisgarh area. They form also prominent bands of highly compressed rocks of the Aravalli ranges from Delhi and Ajmer and also developed in Godavari valley, Bijawar and Gwalior. The aggregate thickness of Cuddapah system is the 6000 m. Undoubted representatives of the Cuddapah system are not recognized in the Himalaya, but it is probable that the basal parts of the Dogra, Attock and Simla slates are of Cuddapah affinities.

Except for building stones and asbestos vein, Cuddapah system is devoid of mineral of commercial utility.

Vindhyan System

Rocks of this system rest upon the denuded surface of the Cuddapahs. Typical development of this system is in Vindhaya mountain, and their outcrop stretches from Aravallies to the Son river valley. The rocks are divisible into lower Vindhyan, and upper Vindhyan, separated by unconformity. Though they are eminently fitted for preservation of fossils the rocks which are wholly of marine organs are completely barren of any organic remains, though it is probable that both animal and vegetable life was in existence on earth during this age. Few representatives of Vindhyan system occur in the Peninsula, south of Narmada, except in patches in Kurnool, Guntur and Bijapur districts. The most important mineral occurrence of the Vindhyan is the diamond pebbles containing both gem and industrial variety are found in some conglomerate beds in the upper Vindhyans. The next important product of this systems—an unlimited stock of excellent building stones suitable for public and monumental buildings – sandstones, limestone, and slate, as well as materials for lime and cement.

The famous buildings of Fethapur Sikri, the Red Fort and government buildings, the Parliament House, North and South Blocks and the Presidential house in Delhi are some of the recent buildings which have used sandstones quarried from Vindhyan group.

In the western India – Rajasthan state, all most all major forts and palaces have used sandstone of this group – to name again, the Umaid Bhawan Palace of Jodhpur and the Mehrangarh Fort. In fact most of the houses in the district of Jodhpur are built by sandstones of this upper Vindhyan group the trans-Aravalli Vindhyan – (now called the Marwar group) (Fig. 9 A and B) and extensively use granite slabs (Fig. 10A and B, and sometimes marble slabs for flooring (Fig. 11).

Palaeozoic (Cambrian to Lower Carboniferous Systems)

After the emergence of the Vindhyan strate from the sea, the peninsula of India, the whole of Deccan south of latitude 28°N remained a stable land area without experiencing any geological disturbance, such as submergence under the sea, folding and mountain building, etc. for a period of several hundred million years, Rock of the upper Vindhyan system have therefore retained their original horizontal bedding.

For the geological record of the succeeding post – Vindhyan ages, one has to go to the extra Peninsular region (the Himalayan) and the area is Kashmir, Spiti, Garhwal–Kumaun, and northeast. Here representatives of marine formation belonging of the Cambrian, Ordovician, Silurian, Devonian, and Lower Carboniferous are preserved in detached outcrops. These systems are fossiliferous and their geological age is easily

Fig.9A & B: Quarring of Sandstone and cutting in West Rajasthan

determined by their fossil content, correlating them to the worlds standard Paleozoic group.

A continuous sequence of strata, generally containing typical fossils (Trilobites, Brachiopods, Corals etc.), commencing from the Cambrian upto Lower Carboniferous, has been met with in Spiti (Himachal Pradesh) and Kashmir (in the Lidar valley) etc. A parallel group, representative of these ages, occurs in Simla, Garhwal, Kumaon, and in North East–Assam–Arunachal Pradesh. It needs to be mentioned that since these rocks do not contain fossils, their correlation in uncertain.

The Himalaya–extra Peninsula part area, together with the adjoining region of Tibet, Burma, Hazara remained submerged under the sea in isolated basin for the greater part of the Palaeozoic times.

Gondwana System

With the beginning of Upper Carboniferous, a series of earth movements encompassing the whole earth took place and affected the course of geological history differently in the extra Peninsula and the Deccan region. In the north, a wide continuous sea (the sea of Telhys) extended from the western Mediterranean to China and remained prominent feature of the Mesozoic geography of the earth till end of Cretaceous. In the south, a large continent (encompassing) Africa, India, and Australia, emerged as result of the earth movements. This southern continent which is known in geology as Gondwanaland, also included parts of south America and Australia.

A series of terrestrial and fluviatile deposits laid down on the surface of this vast continent in a chain of faulted basins constitute the geological record of this part of the world from Upper Carboniferous to the Cretaceous period. Together in the same time with these Gondwanaland – deposits of the south were being laid down in the northern sea borderning the extra Peninsula marine fossiliferous deposits. Hence, a dual facies (facies indicates two different aspects of

Fig. 10A: Mining of Granite block

Fig. 10B: Granite slab after polishing

the same rock formation at different location) of geological formation from the Permian to the Cretaceous exist in India a terrestrial facies containing remains of fossil plants and in the Deccan, and a marine facies containing fossils ammonites, and molluscs in the Himalayan, during the Permian, Triassic, Jurassic and Cretaceous periods.

Gondwana system thus separated a period of Upper Carboniferous to Lower Cretaceous. This system of formations started with a Glacial age (Talchir) during which the area of India from Rajasthan to the Godavari river valley was covered under glacial ice. This was succeeded by a great thickness of sandstones and shales enclosing seams of coal, containing fossil plants indicating a succession of fossil flora. This coal age of India (Damuda) is coeval with the Permian of Europe. The next series, overlying the Damuda, are the Panchet and Mahadeva series of Central India, devoid of coal, but containing remain of Labyrinthodonts and reptiles, in addition to plant remains. The succeeding Gondwana stages are Maleri and Kota, carrying the bones and skeletons of dinosaurs and other reptiles as well as fish remains. The top bed of the Upper Gondwana system occur in Jabalpur and in Kutch, containing fossil belonging to the higher plant life of the periods – e.g. Conifers, succeeding the ferns, which predominated the lower Gondwana.

Economically the lower Gondwana system of rocks is the highest importance to India, as in its strata encloses valuable deposits of coal. The coal fields of eastern India – Bengal – Chota Nagpur, Damodar River region and Mahanadi river region of Odisha, extending west to Chhattisgarh and Madhya Pradesh to Maharashtra contain huge reservers of coal. From building stone view – the holy and famous Temple of Lord Jagannath in Puri is built with sandstones quarried from Gondwana system of rock.

Upper Carboniferous and Permian System Rocks of Himalayas

These rocks are found mostly developed in Kashmir, and Spiti region. They form the base of thick sequence of marine fossiliferrous strata belonging to the Mesozoic period's up to the end to the Cretaceous, deposited on the floor of the Tethys Sea on the north of Gondwanaland. In Kashmir, there is a thick series of volcanic lavas, the Panjal Traps, associated with the characteristics productus – bearing limestone. In the rest of the Himalaya in the Simla, Garhwal, through Nepal in the middle Himalaya, these systems are widely developed, but are totally unfossiliferrous.

Triassic System

Triassic rock is a fossiliferrous limestone, containing a rich ammonite fauna, found in intermittent patches in the middle and northern ranges of the Himalayas forming the Tibetan zone, from Hazara and Kashmir to Assam. Their fossils enable a close correlation of the Himalayan, Trais with Trias of the Alps, and rest of Europe. The Trias of Kumaon, Garhwal designated as the Krol system is unfossiliferrous.

Jurassic System

These rocks overlie the Trias and form a conspicuous horizon, especially in the Tibetan zone of the Himalaya. They show a full development in the Spiti area, but not in Kashmir. Marine Jurassic strata are found in Jaisalmer and Bikaner in Rajasthan containing suits of ammonite fossils. They are also developed in Kutch. Some plant bearing Gondwana beds associated with marine strata have been observed as coastal deposits on the Tamil Nadu coast of Gondwanaland, which by the time had began to disintegrate as an Indo-African continent.

Cretaceous System

A large variety of rock formations belonging to this age are met with in India. On the mid-Deccan plateau, a vast pile of volcanic ash-beds and lava flows, aggregating about 1800 m vertical thickness and covering 300,000 sq km from Mumbai to Nagpur, was formed in the Upper Cretaceous time (Deccan Trap). Cretaceous fluviatile deposits form the top of upper Gondwana beds in some part of the Peninsula. On the Tamil Nadu coast between Puducherry and Tiruchirapalli, there is a well developed upper Cretaceous systems of strata, carrying a varied assemblage of Cretaceous sea-life resting on the ancient Achaean rocks. They also occur in small patches in the Narmada river valley, north Gujarat and Assam, the sandstone horizons of these rocks have been used for building purposes.

At the end of the Cretaceous, the vast Mesozoic continent of Gondwanaland finally broke up and its constituent units either foundered down to give rise to sea-basins, according to one hypothesis, or they drifted away to farm separate distant landmass, according to another view.

Eocene System

This is the dawn of the Tertiary era of earth history. This period defined the present geographical outlines of the Indian Peninsula, after it was separated from Gondwanaland. The commencement of the uplift of the Himalayan chain from the floor of the Tethys sea was another significant event. Typical Eocene rocks are met with in Jammu and Simla sub-Himalaya and also in Assam, as also in Upper Indus basin of Ladakh. The characteristic formation of this age is the foraminiferal nummulitic limestone.

In the Peninsula, the Eocene system is of restricted occurrence. If overlies the Deccan Traps in Kutch, and Cambay, and continues southwards in a string along the Gujarat coast and underneath the shallow Cambay Gulf. In Assam, these rocks cover a large area. The Assam and Gujarat Eocene sequence support the productive oilfields of India.

Fig.11: Marble Block mined out, and its polished surface from Nagaur in Rajasthan

Scattered outcrops of Eocene deposits occur along Coramandal coast, where it is well formed and enclose a thick series of lignite bed. The Neyveli Lignite deposit of Cuddalore belong to this succession.

Eocene are found in western Rajasthan where new oil fields have been located. Eocene rocks occur along Malabar and Coramandal coasts.

Besides petroleum, the big mineral deposit associated with the Eocene rock in India are, coal was in Assam, and lignite in Gujarat and Rajasthan, as well as Tamil Nadu.

Oligocene and Miocene

A thick series of esturine and fluviatile deposits fringing the outer Himalaya of Jammu, Simla-Kangra are products of this age. A Great Boundary Fault separates them from the older formations of the middle and lesser Himalaya. The record prominent uplift of the Himalaya took place during the Miocene. In Assam the rocks of this age overlie the Eocene but in the rest of the Peninsula, the Miocene is poorly developed in Kutch, Kathiawar. (Fig. 6 and 7)

Siwalik System (Middle Miocene- Pleistocene)

The estuarine and fluviatile deposits, mentioned above as being laid down along the foot of the raising mountains, continue to grow all through the period of middle Miocene to lower Pleistocene, from the abundant sediments, supplied by the numerous streams draining the mountain of the north (Himalaya). This system of sandstones, clays, and shales attained a thickness of over 6000 m and entombed in its strata are bones and skeleton of a variety of assemblages of mammals, from primitive elephants to anthropoid apes, some of them on the line of human ancestry. The Siwalik from the outermost foothills of the Himalaya along the entire length from Jammu to Assam.

Pleistocene and Recent

A great refrigeration of climate took place in the northern hemisphere culminating in a glacial age, during which much of Europe and North America were covered under ice-streets. In India, the glacial conditions prevailed only in the Himalaya where evidence of existence of four glacial and inter glacial ages are well recorded in the moraines left by the glaciers and the Karewas deposits of the Kashmir valley.

The Indo-Gangetic Plains

Thick alluvial deposits filled up the great "depression", separating the Himalaya from the Peninsula, which came into being as a concomitant of the Himalayan uplift. This "depression", believed to be between 3000 to 4000 m deep, went on deepening with deposition of thousands of meters of sand, silt, and clays brought down by the river of the Indus–Ganga system. The resulting Indo-Gangetic plain now occupies an area of nearly 500,000 sq km from western parts of India to Assam in the east.

Among the other geological formations of this period are the laterite cap of the Deccan – a product of sub aerial alteration of surface rocks of the Deccan region, raised beaches along the coasts and other coastal deposits; sand dunes, the Cave deposits of Kurnool and more importantly the desert sands which cover a large areas of Rajasthan, Haryana, Gujarat and Kutch.

The soils capping the surface rocks of India, either alluvial or residual, are the most important geological formation, are largely a product of Pleistocene and recent age.

Early man is believed to have appeared in India in about the middle Pleistocene period, about 500,000 years ago from today.

5

Building Stones

In order to be suitable as building stone, a rock should have specific qualities such as capacity to stand the ravages of time and weather, requisite strength to bear strain and superincumbent weight and attractive colour, as also general appearance.

Its structure must also be such as to allow quarrying into good sized blocks or plane. It should possess inherent features such as joints and bedding planes (in sedimentary rocks). It should also be capable of receiving dressing – ordinary or ornamental – without disproportionate test of labour. Susceptibility to weather is an important factor; costly experiments have been made to judge the merits of rocks in this respect. For example, the architects of new India, who required an extensive range of rock material for a variety of purposes, building as well as ornamental, invited the opinion of the Geological Survey of India (GSI) regarding the suitability of the various stones quarried in the neighbouring areas of Rajasthan and Madhya Pradesh. At that time an officer of the GSI was specially deputed to advice on the matter after an examination of various quarries working in these states. The Dharwar System and of equivalents (which carries mainly ore–deposits of the country) is rich in its resources of building material, have various types and colours of granites, marble, limestones, and sandstones, other ornamental building stones and roofing states. The famous marbles which are used in the best specimen of Indian architectures are a product of the system.

The Vindhyan system while not possessing any metalliferrous deposits, is rich in resources of building materials, which furnishes as unlimited measure of excellent and durable free-stone; flagstones, ornamental stones, besides large quantities of limestones for manufacture the manufacturers of lime and cement. The formation known on the Bhandar Stage has yielded material for the building of some of the finest specimens of Indian architecture, the Jalis of Fathepur Sikri near Agra is an example. The famous stupas of Sanchi and Sarnath, the Mughal palaces and mosques of Delhi and Agra and the most of the modern government officers of New Delhi, are built of Vindhyan sandstone. These resources are however, scarely used to their full extent, except in western Rajasthan where the trans-Aravalli Vindhyan (now called the Marwar group) has yielded to build the famous Umaid Bhawan Palace (Chatter Palace – the location where the palace stands and sandstone was quarried) in Jodhpur. Build on a design of the Victoria Memorial of Calcutta, this magnificent palace is situated a top a low ridge, and can be seen from a distance when one approaches the city of Jodhpur. Not only this, the fort of Mehrangarh, just a few kilometer away, but located on a higher hillock, gives equal magnificence. The Mehrangarh fort was built in 400 year ago is older than the Umed Bhawan Palace.

The building for dwelling in Jodhpur and small villas are made of sandstones of this upper Vindhyan time. Their dark red-brown colour, and buff colour gives the designer a grand colour contrast is construction material.

In recent years – buildings of modern India have greatly utilized sandstones, marbles, flagstone, granite and serpentinized ultramafic, the black dolerites, gabbro and syenites

– the porphyry as the most expensive and extensive buildings stones. The Delhi Metro stations have made the full use of granite slabs for platform stairs and so on.

GRANITES

Granite, or what passes by that name, is coarsely foliated gneiss. Of its three varieties namely biotite-granite, hornblende granite, and tourmaline–granite, biotite granite is most widely prevalent and forms a very suitable building stone for durability and decoration. These rocks, by the reason of their massive nature and homogeneous grains are adopted for monumental and architectural rock, as well as for massive masonries. Their wide range in appearance and colour, white, pink, red, gray, black etc. renders the stone slightly ornamental and effective for a variety of decorative uses. The charnockites (name given by Sir Thomas Holland after Job Charnock, the founder of Calcutta) of Tamilnadu, the Arcot gneiss, Bangalore gneiss, the porphyries of Serirangpatnan and many other varieties in Madurai region and other districts of the Peninsula are attractive examples. Its durability is such that numerous ancient temples – from Big Temple of Tanjore, to Natraj Temple of Chidamberran, Meenakshi Temple of Maudrai of southern India are built of granite/charnockites stand today almost intact of the centuries of wear and to all appearances, are almost intact today. Form their wide prevalence, forming nearly fourth of the surface of Peninsula, the Archean gneiss form an inexhaustible source of good material for building and ornamental uses. The following major occurrences of granite are noteworthy.

Andhra Pradesh

Granites in Andhra Pradesh have been used in the construction of Nagarjuna Sagar dam, and much earlier in the construction of Bombay Harbour and several public buildings, the Hyderabad granite take the pride of place. The other rocks suitable for construction purpose are the charnockites (used in the constructing Krishna barrage) and Khondalites occurring in the circas.

Assam

Granites and granite gneisses are found throughout the Shillong plateau. Coarse granite around Mylliem and also a few places along the northern scrap of the plateau facing – Golpara, Kamrup and Nowgong plains is being quarried for building stones.

Tamil Nadu

Of the building stones with which the state is richly endowed, granite, gneiss and charnockite are the most widely distributed particularly in North Arcot, Chingleput, Madurai, Ramanatapuram, Tirunelveli and parts of Triuchirapalli and Nilgiri districts.

Karnataka

Building stones are obtained from the surface exposures of granites–gneiss and many other gneiss many of which are remarkably fresh. These gneissic rocks have supplied building material to most of the beautiful structure in Bangalore city.

Odisha

The state has a wide distribution of granite gneiss and khondalities of which the sculptures of the Sun Temple of Konarak is a classic example, the figures having been carved on mottled khondalitic rock and mottled Cuttack sandstone.

Rajasthan

The state has now emerged also as a producer of granite – the Jalore, Siwana, and other granites have received attention for quarrying and the slabs are sold for buildings design.

LIMESTONES

Limstones occur in many formation some of which are entirely composed of them. Not all of them however, are fit for building purposes, though many of them are burnt for lime. The limestone (also called Chuna-ka-Pathar), as its name suggests, is the main source of lime. In earlier times this was used in place of cement and mortar during the time of several forts and palaces. Therefore, we make a special mention of them.

Lime for mortar making is obtained by burning limestone. Lime when mixed with water and sand is called mortar, which when it looses its water and absorbs carbonic acid from air, 'sets' or hardens. Hence it is used as a binding or cement, material. In the plains of India, the only available source of lime is 'kankar' or carbonate concretions, which occur plentiful as irregular concretion disseminated in the clays. The clay admixture in kankar offer sufficient proportion to produce, on burning, a hydraulic lime – call "Tuta" which is often in sufficient proportion to produce – Travertine or calc – "tufa" ("Tufa" is a kind of calcium carbonate). Sea-shell, recent coral limestones, are also used in the kiln where a suitable source of these exists. When limestone containing argillaceous matters in a certain proportion is burnt, the resulting product is cement, in which an altogether different chemical action takes place when mixed with water. The burning of limestone ($CaCO_3$) and clay (xAl_2O_3, y SiO_2, $2H_2O$) together result in the formation of a new chemical component – silicate and aluminate of lime – which again reacts chemically when water is added, hardening it into a dense compact mass. For cement – making, either some suitable clayey limestone is used or more commonly, the ingredients, limestone and clay, are artificially mixed together in proper proportion (portland cement): A high grade rapid hardening cement, rich in aluminous content (cement fondu) used in special structure, can be manufactured from aluminium laterite mixed in approximate quantities of limestone (pig iron is a byproduct of this).

The Eocene system, which is rich in Nummulitic, oolitic, miliolitic and coral limestone, offer favourable condition for cement manufacture. The occurrence of these and other older, limestones in Tamil Nadu, Madhya Pradesh. Rajasthan, Gujarat, Assam and some other parts of India, in association with clays and shell are an asset to the manufacturing of cement. Most kinds of limestone suitable for the purpose occurring in various geological system of India are listed state wise.

Andhra Pradesh

Limestone occur near Borra caves in Visakhapatnam district, in East Godavari district, along banks of river Talperu. Taking of length of 3 km and a width of 100 m, the total quantity available would be about 3-4 million tons of limestones.

Other working deposits of limestone occur in Duddukuru-Rajamundry, area, near Mukteswaran in Krishna dist., in Palnad, Guntur, Cuddapah, Kurnool, Warangal, Karim Nagar, Adilabad, and Khammam districts. The great thickness of limestone shale, and quartzite in Hyderabad and adjoining area provides a prolific source of cement material.

Assam-Meghalaya

The resources of high grade limestone in the region are about the best in the country, although they occur as discontinuous bands along the southern wall of Garo, Khasi, Jaintia, and Mikir hills, the quantity being enormous. Individual bands at places vary from 15 to 40 m in thickness. Fairly good quality limestone also occurs in the North Cachar hills and the parts of Mikher hills bordering Nowgong and Sibsagar districts. The total resource is estimated to be about 154 millin tons. In Khasi hills, Therrighat area itself contains a resource of about 1000 million tons of good quality of limestone.

Gujarat

High grade limestone occur near Pasural, Diwania, Khunia and Viaromudi in Pabanpur subdistrict of Banaskanta district, near Chorwad Road Railway station, Kunderva, Adri Road Railway station, Dari, Veraval Savni, Patan, Hati, Govokhundi, Prachi, Suttapara, and Warodra in Janagarh district. Extensive deposits of good quality limestone occur near Posina, north of Idar in Sabarkantha district. Other occurrences are near Balasinor in Khara district near Lunawada in Panchmahals. Extensive deposits of oolitic limestone occur in region surrounding Bhuj- such as those seen near Jura, Habo and other domes. Also in Kutch in areas near Keerai are good quality deposits. Yellow and slightly porous nummulitic limestone, occur in Surat district is a cement grade, and it is estimated to have a reserve of 3 million ton. Isolated small pockets of travertine occur near Chinchinageotha, Satpuria, and Dhodra in Dang district.

Miliolitic limestone occurs in coastal areas and Kodinar and Okha Mandal in Jamnagar district. Fairly good quality of miliolitic limestone in seen near Paperla Sanosra, Chogal Mehtla, Naip, Gujarda Khard, and Nisaud in Bhavnagar District.

Coral limestone occur along the coastal margins of Okha Mandal. The deposit near Mithapur alone is reported to contain about 5 million tons of coral limestone. The deposit near Gora – Bhilwasi – Tejpur areas are of low grade.

Himachal Pradesh

High grade limestones have been reported from Sirmur district (Naura, Bhangari, and Jarang), the quantity at Naura alone exceed 170 million tons. There are suitable occurrences also in Giri river in Sirmur district near Sataun, Bhatrog, and Kyori. Reserves of these are about 141 million tones. Overlying there is the Mandhili limestone, the average composition of which is probably similar to that of natural cement rock, the reserves of which also run into several million tons. Limestone deposits also reported from Khadli and Kakarhatti, in Mahasy district. Remoteness of some occurrences from industries centres and lack of communication, however, lessen their importance.

Jammu and Kashmir

Limestone suitable for manufacturing 'portland' cement occurs in large quantity in Ramban, Kistwar, Doda, Ramsu, Handwara, Kaghan, Banihal, Vihi, Verang, Zamalgam – Tserkar – Doru – Naupura belt, Achhibal and Bawan in Anantnag district, and Bandipura, Ajas, Gung-i-Sudarkut, Biru and Sonamarg – Zoji La. Though the great limestone of Riasi area in Jammu region in mostly dolomitic, a thick and consistent band low in magnesia has been located recently.

Jharkhand

Limestone deposits occur in Shahabad, Hazaribagh, Ranchi, Palamau and Singhbhum districts. Those of Shahabad district are traceable for about 60 km and extend further west-ward beyond the state. The Rohtas limestones of Shahabad district are especially valuable as they are extensively drawn upon for burning as well as for building purposes. Large patches of limestone occur scattered over a zone extending from Ramgarh, in Hazaribagh to Khalari, Bhundu-Basaria, Kukata and Religara. Deposits of Bisaria and theose of Daltonganj in Palamu region and around Gola and Sondimara in Hazaribagh area are amongst the many new occurrences that have recently being discovered. A 45 km belt of limestone extends from Chaibasa to Jagannathpur in Sighbhum District.

Kerala

Lime-shell deposits occur near Puthur in Kasargod part of Cannanore district. The shelly layers which occur at a depth of 1 to 4 m from the surface has a thickness of 20 to 60 cm and is workable during post monsoon time every year.

A large deposit of lime shell occurring at Vembanad lake, Kottayan and counstitutes the source for lime for the cement industry in the state. Limestone of fairly good quality is exposed in the coastal cliff section in various places in Kollam. Kankar (concretion of calcium carbonate) limestone occurs at places in Palghat district. It is high in magnesia but is suitable for lime-burning. Important deposits of Kankar are also present in Chittur area of Palghat district near Attampathy, whose average thickness is about 7 m.

Madhya Pradesh and Chhattisgarh

Limestone occurs in districts of Jabalpur, Raigarh, Raipur, Bilaspur, Durg, Bastar, Sagar, Damoh, Reva, etc. and is quarried on a large scale, particularly at Katni, and near Jabalpur and Jukehi near Jabalpur, Alaktana (Bilaspur) and also near Raipur. At Katni limestone is quarried mainly for producing lime. Dolomite (dolomitic limestone, calcium, magnesium carbonate) is exposed at Bhanesar, Parsub, Khaira, Ramtola and Hardia in Bilaspur district.

Tamil Nadu

Limestone suitable for the manufacture of 'portland' cement occur in Tiruchinapalli district. Other suitable crystalline limestone occurs at Salem in Coimbatore, Madurai and Tirunelveli districts. The deposits at Tiruichinapalli, Coimbatore, and Tirunelveli districts are under active exploitation for cement manufacture while these in Ramanathan-puram are now being exploited. Tufaceous (limestone), which may be used for manufacture of lime, occur extensively in Tirunelveli, Tanjore and south Arcot districts. Kankar is of common occurrence in Tamil Nadu, and is widely used by rural population for manufacture of lime.

Maharashtra

Fine grained gray limestone occur at Purukepur in Chanda district, and near Kondara, Mardha and Niljai. Fairly good quality deposit occur at Majri and Wanjri near Rajpur railway station in Yeotmal district. Calcareous tufa containing over 75% $CaCO_3$ occur near Kamur, Kandur and Khandera Vadi in Ahmednagar district.

Karnataka

Material for cement work in the state are drawn from Shahabad and Wadi Limestone in Gulbanga district, the quarries of Bhadigund and the crystalline limestone of Shimoga, Chitradurga, Tumkur, and Mysore districts. Occurrence at Hosadurga and Vablapur in Chitradurga and Tumkur districts respectively are known to contain about 50 million tons of limestone averaging 3 to 4 percent of silica, 49 percent of lime and 2.8 percent of magnesia.

Odisha

Limestone of Sambalpur district is argillaceous, siliceous and dolomitic. Limestone suitable for cement manufacture is found near Kottametta in Korapur district as in the long belt of Lanjibera near Rajangpur. Limestone has been quarried around Birmitrapur since 1922. Assuming a total length of 6.4 km, an average width of 225 m. and a depth of 30 m, the quantity of limestone here is estimated at 37 million tons. Of this 25 percent may be classed as useful for lime burning.

Punjab and Himachal Foothill

Limestone occur in a discontinuous belt at the fringe of the foot hills on the north-eastern border of the state. In this belt between Tundapather and Sheria, a reserve of 26 million ton of limestone has been estimated. The quarries at Malla provide rich cement material. Small deposits of lime concentrate known as calc-tufa occur near Samal god extending into Kangra district of Himachal Pradesh. Hoshiarpur district limestones occur at Beranpur, Kherakalmot and Lehra.

Rajasthan

Limestone suitable for manufacture of portland cement is obtained from Ajmer, Banswara, Bikaner, Dungarpur, Jodhpur, Kota, Tonk, and Udaipur district, and in the vicinity of Swai Madhopur and Lakhari in Bundi districts. Calcite is also reported from Maonda and Raipur in Sikar district, Paparana in Jhunjhunu district, Basna-ki-chowki and Sakhoon in Jaipur District, and Rajpura in Sirohi district.

Uttrakhand

Limestone occur in Tons valley in Amlawa, and Yamuna rivers in the Chakrata area. Tufa deposits occur in Nanital, vicinity of Dehra Dun.

Uttar Pradesh

Kankar is found in various places. Limestone occur in Markundi and Kotah in Mirzapur district.

West Bengal

Calcareous tufa containing more than 45 percent of $CaCO_3$, found in Darjeeling district of western Duars area in Jalpaiguri, district is a source of lime material. Local concentration of carbonate concretions developing in parts of the soils of Ranigunj coal fields in Burdwan, Bankura, and other district being fairly wide in lime content, provide material for lime making.

Stone from two highly siliceous discontinuous bands of crystalline limestone along the northern flank of the hills near Ichata and Jhabar near Jhalda and places in Purulia district is used for manufacture of low grade lime.

LIMESTONES AS A BUILDING STONE

Limestones suitable as building stone occur in large quantity and in several places, but the best limestone occur in Vindhyan systems of rocks.

In the Cuddapah, Bijawar, Khonolite and Aravalli groups, limestone attain considerable development, some of them being of great beauty and strength. They have been largely drawn upon in the construction of many of the noted monuments of the part in all parts of the country. As mentioned above, Vindhyan limestones are extensively quarried in Rajasthan and form a source of building stone as valued as that of lime and cement mentioned earlier.

The Gondwana spread over large parts of Jharkhand and Madhya Pradesh, and Chhattisgarh, are known of calcareous rocks, but the small exposes of the Bagh and Tiruchirapalli Cretaceous include excellent limestone, sometimes even of an ornamental description. The same is the case with limestone of lower Vindhyan formation which is also extensively drawn upon for building as well as for burning purpose. The great thickness of limestone together and with shades and series quartzite, constituting the Palnad series of Hyderabad and adjoining areas, shows local variations in the rock types, but principally conforms to the argillaceous and calcareous nature of the system. Some of the limestones show a concretionary structure, the concentric layers exhibiting are giving to the polished rock a marble like appearance. At some places, on the coast of Saurashtra, a kind of coastal deposit occur, known as Porbander stone, also called miliolite. It is composed of calcareous wind blown sand, and sand grains being largely made of the caste of foraminifera, the whole compacted into a kind of white or cream coloured, rudely bedded free-stone. The rock known as Junagarh limestone is a typical aeolian limestone situated 50 km inland from the sea coasts and 60 meters thick. It is mainly composed of fragments of calcareous shells most of them living species, cemented by lime. About 6 to 12 percent of foreign particles of Girnar igneous rock enter into the composition. It is believed that Saurashtra than stood 50 feet (15 m) lower than its present level and was probably in Pleistocene time as inland or groups of island.

From their softness and the ease with which they receive dressing and ornamental treatment, these limestone are a favourite material for architectural purposes in western Indian states, specially in Maharashtra. Crystalline limestone, marble-like in appearance is reported to occur at Sandara in the Sankhada Mahal near Ther, Mithibor, Kendol, Chetapur, Melu, and Bhilpur in Chhota Udepur Taluk in Baroda district and between Hansi and Shir in Bharueh district. Limestones from Shahabed, Wadi and places in Gulbarga district of Karnataka are widely used. They take good polish and make suitable medium for flagstones, roofstones and building material in general.

The Nummulitic limestones of the extra Peninsula (Himalaya) in Himachal Pradesh, Assam, Meghalaya are enormous repository of pure limestone and when accessible are in large demand for building as well as for burning and road making purposes.

MARBLES

Marble deposits of India are fairly widespread and of large extent. The principal source of the marbles in the crystalline formation of Rajasthan – the Aravalli group – marble quarries are worked at Makrana, Kharwa, Maundla, and Bhainslana, Dadikar (Alwar) and some other places from where marbles of many varities of colour and grain including the chaste, while variety of which the Taj Mahal is built are obtained. It was the accessibility of this store of material of unsurpased beauty which, no doubt, gave a stimulus to the Moghul taste of architecture in the seventeenth century.

A sacchroidal dolomitic (dolomite is magnesian limestone) marble occur in a large outcrop near Jabalpur, where it is traversed by the Narmada gorge (These well known marble rock occur about 18 km from Jabalpur and is a well known tourist attraction.

The famous quarries of Makrana supply white, gray, and pink marbles. A handsome pink marble comes from village Narimada in Kishangarh district (which lies close to Ajmer city) in Rajasthan.

Jaisalmer in Rajasthan supplies a yellow sheddy marble, while a fresh-green and mottled marble of exquisite finish is obtained from Motipura from an exposure of the Aravalli rocks in Baroda district in Gujarat state. A mottled rose or pink marble is found in the same locality and in one or two places in the Aravalli group in Rajasthan, and in Narsingpur district of Madhya Pradesh, whereas white mottled hard from near Khirasra Sejridle in Gujarat state is of ornamental value. The Kharwa quarries of Ajmer produce green and yellow coloured marbles. Black or dark coloured marble come from Makrana and from Kishangarh district, through their occurrence is of a more limited scale than the high coloured verities. A dense, black marble capable of taking exquisite polish, largely employed in ancient buildings of Delhi, Agra and Kashmir with highly ornamental effect is furnished by some quarries in Jaipur region. Coarse grained marbles are more suitable for architectural and monumental uses; it is the coarseness of the grains which is the cause of its great durability against meteoric weathering. The fine grained present white variety marble is reserved for statuary use which no other variety can serve.

In the Tiruchinapalli region, the shell limestone has compacted into a hard – fine grained translucent stone which is much prized as an ornamental stone and used in construction under the name of "Trichinapoly' marble.

Black and white marbles were, at one time, worked in Mandi and Datla hills of Narnaul Tehsil an Mahendergarh district of Haryana. It is disappointing though, that these deposits do not find any market so as to encourage their systematic quarrying. The indigenous demand is not considerable nor are there any facilities for their export, the deposits, therefore, perhaps will have to wait the demand of a more thriving and more aesthetic population. It may be relevant to add here for those interested in variety of marbles in India, a good collection of Indian marbles of several variations are displayed in the garden of the Indian Museum in Kolkata.

SANDSTONES

The Vindhyan group of rocks, through not possessing any metalliferous deposits, is as rich of repository of sandstone and limestone as indicated earlier. It furnishes unlimited, durable and attractive building material such as freestones, flagstones, ornamental stones, besides large quantities of limestones for manufacture of lime and cement as mentioned earlier.

The "Bhander stage" has yielded materials for building stones of the finest speciments of the Indian architecture. The famous stupas of Sanchi and Sarnath, the Mughal palaces and mosques of Delhi and Agra and the modern government buildings of New Delhi capital zone are built of Vindhyan sandstones. The most prominent amongst these are the white, cream, buff and pink varieties.

Upper Vindhyan Sandstones, which have been put to an almost inconceivable number of projects. The crude stone knives and scraps of the Paleolithic man to the railway, telegraph, and the exquisitely carved monoliths of its present day successor, these sandstones have supplied for infinity of uses. It is the most widely quarried stone in India. Being both a freestone and a flagstone, it can yield, depending on the position selected, both gigantic blocks for pillars and thin slate-like slabes for paving and roofing. The superb edifices, modern and medieval in Delhi, Agra and Rajasthan are built of red and white Vindhyan sandstone quarried from a number of sites in the vicinity. Some of the Vindhyan sandstones are so homogeneous and soft that they are capable of receiving a most elaborate carving and filigree work. Centered of exposure to the weather have tested they durability. An early as 1881, Dr. V. Ball of the Geological Survey of India (Economic Geology LIII). "The difficulty in writing of the uses to which these rocks have been put is not in finding examples, but in selecting from the numerous ancient and modern buildings which crowd the cities of Uttar Pradesh and Ganga Valley generally and in which the stone-cutters art in seen in the highest perfection".

The Vindhyan sandstones uniformly fine grained in their variegated shades are sometimes mottled or speckled owning to the variable dissemination of the colouring matter or to its removal by de-oxidation The Kaimur and Bhandar Sandstones of deep-red tint pursuing now and then into softer, elegant shades are remarkable, and make easy quarrying. No other rock formation of India possesses such an assemblage of character, rendering it so eminently suitable for building or architecture application. When thinly stratified, the rock yields flags, or slabs, when the bedding is coarse the rock yields large blocks and columns.

The sandstones obtained in Saurashtra (Jurassic outcrops is North-east) is a light coloured free stones, largely quarried at Dhrangadhra for supplying various parts of Gujarat with a needed building material.

NEWER SANDSTONES

To a lesser extent the Gondwana formations affort sandstones suited for building works. The Upper Gondwana has contributed a great store of building-stone to Odisha and Chhattisgarh regions. The famous temple of Puri and other richly ornamated buildings of these districts are constructed of upper Gondwana sandstone. The fine-grained sandstones of Cuttack, Athgarh, Tirupati are much used for structure purposes. The Mesozoic (Umia) sandstone of Dhrangadhra and the Cretaceous sandstone underlying the "Bagh beds" of Gujarat (example Songir sandstone) furnish Gujarat with a handsome and durable medium for its building construction.

Among the Tertiary sandstones only a few possess the quality requisite in a building stone, whereas the younger Siwalik sandstone is all too unconsolidated and incoherent to be a medium of construction.

LATERITE

Laterite is the product of a peculiars sub-aerial alteration of surface rocks under the alternately dry and humid (e.g. monsoonic) weather of India. Laterite is a kind of vesicular, clayey rock, composed essentially of mixture of the hydrated oxide of aluminium and iron with often a small parentage of other oxide chief among which are manganese and titanium oxides. The term "laterite" has been derived from the Latin word "later" meaning a brick.

Laterite is largely used as a building stone, as it is a widespread Pleistocene surface formation of considerable extent and thickness. It has the peculiar property of being soft when newly quarried but becomes hard and compact when exposed to the air. On account of this property, it is usually cut in the form of bricks for building purposes.

Loosened fragments and pebbles of thick rock tend to re-cement themselves into solid masses as compact as original rock.

Distribution

Laterite occurs principally as a cap on the summit of the basaltic hill, and plateaus of the highlands of the Deccan, Rajasthan, Madhya Pradesh and Eastern India. In its best and most typical development it occurs of the hills of Mumbai. In all these situation it is found capping the highest flows of the Deccan Traps (basalts) Laterite is by no means confined to the Deccan area but is found to extent in isolated outcrops as far north as the Rajmahal hills of Jharkhand state to the southern extremity of the Peninsula. It extends further to Sri Lanka where it is forms a thick up covering the gneiss and the Khondalites.

In the north east, laterite cover cochar region, in the basal parts of the Jaintia series, the Garo, Khasi, and Jaintia hills.

In several parts of southern India, laterite is quarried for use as a building stone since it can be easily cut into bricks, but is not capable of receiving dressing for any architectural or ornamental use. Moreover, its wide distribution from NE to Cape Comorin makes laterite a widely used material for road metal.

The famous church of old Goa is a beautiful examples of use of laterite in building purposes. Goa has several buildings made of laterite stones.

SLATES

Slates are one of the units forming the bulk of the Dharwar and Aravalli groups as also Cuddapah group of rocks. Besides its use as the familiar writing slate, switch boards and tabletops, when split suitably, it is used as a roofing material, and paving and shelves. The true cleavage slate which is the roofing and paving variety of slates, is not of common occurrence in India, except in mountain areas of Kumaun and Simla, Mandi, Chamba as also in Pir Panjal in Kashmir Himalaya. It is a good roofing material obtainable locally for hill town and village.

Extensive beds occur in Cumbum – Markapur area in Kurnool district where slate making is a cottage industry. Slate occurs in Cuddapah area inters bedded with iron and manganese ores. Large deposits occur in Dhauladhar range near Dharmsala in

Kangra district and in vicinity of Rewari– Narnaul in Haryana, in the Aravallis and in Kharagpur hills in Monghyr (Bihar).

About 60 percent of the Indian slate production comes from Himachal Pradesh and Haryana. When the cleavage in slate is finely developed and regular, enabling the rock to be split into their even plates, roofing slates are available, when the cleavage is not fine slate is used for paving. What generally are called slates are either phyllite or compacted shales in which the planes of splitting are not cleavage planes.

BASALTS

The rock basalt is largely spread in the Deccan – Maharashtra, and surrounding slates. Therefore, these basalts are known as Deccan Traps, as sub-aerial, volcanic product, prevailing over a wide region of western India. These basalts are mostly used by the Railway and Public Works Departments for building bridges, permanent ways etc. basalts or Trap... furnish easily workable and durable stones of great strength but its dull, subduced colour does not find it as a popular use. Nonetheless some magnificent buildings of Pune, the University office (earlier British resident house) and several buildings are standing to show strength and consequences of traps as a building stone. The Taj Hotel in Mumbai is another outstanding example of use of traps as a building stone.

Acidic lavas such as Trachyes

Recent change in choice of light buff and cream colours stone have made them attractive. They occurr for commerce at Malad near Mumbai have found favour in the building of public edifices.

Sylhet Traps

Like the Deccan Traps, the Sylhet Traps of Khasi, Jaintia and Mikir hills of the north east India especially in Koilajam area, Jamuna, Hariajan and Deopatic river beds and some near Nambor water falls, in Abor hills of Arunachal Pradesh are found useful for road making and concrete mixture. The Khasi greenstones in the Shillong plateau are useful for making shelves slabs in homes.

GNEISS (the famous Basement Gneisses)

The oldest of gneisses are quarried extensively in parts of Rajasthan for use as building stone at percent, and which has been the medium of construction of Temples of western India.

The present day annual average value of building stone output of in India is a big, and is growing rapidly.

Large quantity of gneisses from Peninsula (Karnataka, Andhra Pradesh, and Tamilnadu) are quarried, polished and sold as interior of the houses and apartments.

6

Recorded Cultural Diversity

SARNATH

Let us take ourselves back in history and visit a monument that is intimately related to spiritual figure who is revered even in the modern day world. His teachings and philosophy has brought tranquility and peace to millions both now and before.

Sarnath near Varanasi (Benaras) is a park created by Emperor Ashoka in the third century BC and it is where Gautama Buddha taught his first lesson of Buddhism after attaining his enlightenment at Bodh Gaya. It became one of the foremost monastery of Buddhism until 1194 AD when Qutubuddin Aibak, the Muslim conqueror levelled the place and Sarnath remained buried under the rubble. However, the excavations discovered the nearly intact Dharmekha stupa seen in the background on the right which has been thought to be built by Ashoka (Fig. 12). This stupa is a very sacred place for Buddhist and it represents a symbol of enlightened mind. HH Dilgo Khyenste Rinpoche said that, "When a great teacher passes away, his body is no more, but to indicate that his

Fig.12: The Sarnath, Varanasi

mind is dwelling forever in an unchanging way in the dharmakaya, one will erect stupa as a symbol of the mind of the buddha's".

The original Dharmekha stupa was built by Ashoka and the present height of the Stupa is 31 metres. The lower portion of the Stupa is covered by beautifully carved stones. The carving (Fig. 13) shows a broad band of interwoven swastikas flanked at the top and bottom by lotus carvings. This stupa is one of the indications that the swastika was a symbol of 'peace' and was widely used before it was usurped by the Nazis making it a symbol of hatred. The lotus on the other hand has all along been a symbol of spiritual offering dating back from centuries. The photo shows marks of pillage that the Stupa suffered silently over centuries but remained a beacon for enlightenment.

Fig. 13: Carving on Stupa in Sarnath, Varanasi

Fig.14: Qutub Minar –
A little bit higher and a little bit ancient

QUTUB MINAR

From Sarnath we bring ourselves forward in history where the stones took another dimension based on the culture of the builders who erected this monument and is a fine example of an 'Indo-Islamic architecture. It is the Qutab Minar.

A sandstone arch frames the famous Qutab Minar in Delhi (Fig. 14: Qutub Minar). Made of "Vindhyan" red sandstone, its foundation was laid by the first Muslim sultan of Delhi, King Qutubuddin Aibak in 1199 hailing from Afghanistan to commemorate the victory over the last Hindu king Prithiviraj Chauhan in 1192. The minaret, built by stages is 72.9 metres high and is embellished with inscriptions in Arabic illustrating the history of the rise of Qutab Minar from 1199 to 1370.

The photograph (Fig. 14) depicts the remnants of Hindu temple carvings found at the base of the Qutab Minar, indicating the presence of a Hindu temple complex that initially occupied this site and remains a witness to the fall of the Hindu empire and the start of the Muslim rulers.

The photograph (Fig. 15A and B) shows the art of stone carvings has not died in India and the attempts to restore some of the damaged stones with the same red sandstone found locally is a sign of the willingness to preserve the cultural heritage of India.

LODHI MAUSOLEUM

If we take a walk right in the midst of the city of New Delhi we come across a series of structures that evoke the blending of architectural design of octagonal shape and curving domes reminiscent of Muslim, Hindu as well as east European imprint, again using local stones. We focus our attention to the Lodhi Mausoleum

Fig.15A: Qutub Minar – The witness

Fig.15B: Qutub Minar –
The challenge to reproduce the ancient work of art

During the last of the dynasty of Pathan rulers from Afghanistan, the Lodhis, there was a proliferation of tombs honouring the death of nobles from that period compared to say the Hindu or the Mughal periods. According to some, this could be interpreted as a premonition of the destruction of the short lived Lodhi dynasty. The octagonal tomb (Fig. 16) is that of Sikandar Lodhi, showing the natural beauty of the sandstone reflecting the setting sun (Fig. 17) or the majestic stone staircase leading up to the tomb (Fig. 18) and we can see the mixture of what could be an inspiration from the Hindu architecture depicting elephant trunks (Fig. 19), uncommon to the Muslim architecture.

The period of British rule saw the transformation of the area of tombs by addition of well laid out gardens making it a favourite landmark not only of the tourists but the local population of Delhi as well.

Fig. 16: Lodhi Mausoleum – Immortalizing a dynasty

Fig. 17: Lodhi Mausoleum – Corridor of history

Fig. 18: Lodhi Mausoleum – The steps of time

Fig. 19: Lodhi Mausoleum – Pure or hybrid art?
Lodhi Museum, Part or hybrid art?

FATEHPUR SIKRI

From the Lodhi mausoleum we transpose ourselves to a period where the stones played a major role in preserving the history and culture of the Mughal dynasty which left an indelible imprint on the all spheres of the Indian life. We are talking about Emperor Akbar's erudition and Emperor Shah Jahan's immortal poetry of love through the use of stones as seen through Fatehpur Sikri and the Taj Mahal.

We are at Fatehpur Sikri, 26 miles west of the city of Agra. It was a royal city built by the famous Mughal Emperor Akbar, starting in 1571 (Fig. 20). Akbar was a very tolerant ruler and Fatehpur Sikri reflects this since it blends both Islamic and Hindu architecture

Fig. 20: Fatehpur Sikri – Benediction

Fig. 21: Fatehpur Sikri – Harmony on a large scale

Fig. 22: Fatehpur Sikri – I see you but you don't see me

Fig. 23: Fatehpur Sikri – A splendid secret

(Fig. 21). The main palace was built mostly with "Vindhyan" red sandstone as well as marble. However, after its completion in 1586, the city had to be abandoned because of shortage of water. A witness to the Muslim culture are the sandstone and marble screens (Fig. 22-23) through which the women could look out and not being seen.

TAJ MAHAL

The most magnificent use of stones is the offering of the Mughal Emperor Shah Jahan as a witness to his love for his favourite wife, Arjumand Banu Begum (better known as Mumtaz) who died in childbirth in 1629. The Taj Mahal, started in 1631 on the banks of river Jamuna in Agra, took twenty years to build. The saddest part of the story is that these stones made to radiate the beauty of the deceased beloved became a silent witness to the pain of Shah Jahan. Culturally, the Mughal Empire was beset with jealousy and the thirst for power. A younger son of Shah Jahan, Aurangzeb, who was not a natural successor to the throne, imprisoned his Father and proclaimed himself as the emperor.

Fig. 24: Taj Mahal – Ô My beloved Mumtaz, you are so far away

Fig. 25: Taj Mahal – Stones, moon and the sky

Fig. 26: Mumtaz, the stones evoke your beauty

Shah Jahan, instead of being in close communion with his beloved's tomb, had to satisfy himself by gazing at the mausoleum from the Agra Fort (Fig. 24) where he was imprisoned.

The marble, from Makrana in Rajasthan, takes its hue from the rays of the sun and the light of the moon. No effort was spared to use semi-precious stones brought in from faraway places to build one of the wonders of the Muslin architecture with its carvings, base relief and inlay work. (Figs. 25-26)

Being such a stately structure, the Taj Mahal was the focus of pillage and vandalism through history by later rulers and the marble has been fighting a silent battle against its deterioration from the industrial air pollution of the present time.

GOLCONDA

The Muslim rulers not only occupied the northern part of the country but had a far reaching grip in the South of India as well

Fig. 27: Golconda – The protector

Fig. 28: Golconda – Illuminating our heritage

Fig. 29: Golconda – Flying towards the Mosque

Fig. 30: Golconda – Do you think we can see the wall from space?

The presence of Muslim rulers in South India is best exemplified by the Golconda fortress complex near Hyderabad. The site of the fortress was a natural choice where immense granitic rocks produced a natural relief on the "Deccan Plateau" a stable rock formation like the "Canadian Shield". The original fort was built of mud by the Hindu Kakatiya King in the 13th century. From 1507, over a period of 62 years The Qutub Shahi Sultans (the Pathans from Afghanistan), took over the fort and completely reconstructed it using the granites from the hill and incorporating the huge *in situ* boulders as a part of the fortification (Fig. 27). The fort took a distinct Muslim flavour, with vaulted arches (Fig. 28), mosques with minarets (Fig. 29). The pink granite was used for constructing kilometres of ramparts (Fig. 30). Alas! The Mughal Emperor Auragazheb captured the fort and left it in ruins.

KONARAK

We now go back in time and feel ourselves fortunate that the builders used the local rocks which stood up to the natural weathering processes since the structure is not far from the sea and the landward wind is charged with water and salt. We are alluding to the Konarak Sun Temple.

Dating back from centuries stones have preserved the identity the Hindu culture in the form of temples and sculptures. One of the greatest example is the sun temple of Konarak. It is near the shores of the Bay of Bengal in the State of Odisha. Built by the Hindu king Narasimhadev I, who reigned between 1238-64 AD. The temple is dedicated to the sun god Surya and is in the form of a huge chariot with 12 pairs of wheel and drawn by seven horses (it required 16 years, 1200 artisans and 12000 labourers to complete this magnificent temple) (Figs. 31, 32, 33, 34).

Fig. 31: Konarak – The chariot of Surya, the sun god

Fig. 32: Konarak – Majestic presence

Fig. 33: Konarak – Rolling in search of peace

Fig. 34: Konarak – Pillars of intricate beauty

Local stones were used to construct this temple and they are of a special kind. Called "khondalites" they are metamorphic rocks (rocks tempered by heat and pressure in the interior of the earth) showing patterns due to alignments of minerals like garnet etc) (Fig. 35).

These sculptured stones depict a rich cultural heritage where both human and mythical forms show the power of imagination dating back centuries (Fig. 36). The Hindu symbolism of elephants is very much alive in the Konarak temple along with scenes of daily life and amorous instants (Figs. 37 and 38). The artistic prowess, the patience and time is cost prohibitive in the present time so we see uncarved blocks of the same rock supporting the crumbling pillars and walls put up during present time (Fig. 34). This disintegration is a combination of destruction and pillage by invading armies and the salt laden winds from the sea.

Fig. 35: Konarak – Long before Star Trek

Fig. 36: Konarak – Reality and imagination. Look and you will discover

Fig. 37: Konarak – Bas-relief: we cannot make a mistake with elephants

Fig. 38: Konarak – The beauty of natural stones

JAISALMER

From the South-east of India we travel to the North-West where the rocks resisted both the ravages of time and the onslaught of invaders. We are in the land of Hindu warriors, the Rajputs.

Parallel to the time when Muslim culture was being propagated through stone base architecture, there flourished, palaces, and fortified towns made of stones illustrating the Hindu architectural influence. These structures were put up by Rajputs. They are warriors who populated the States now known as Rajasthan and Madhya Pradesh who resisted the Muslim invasion into their territories and possibly saved these monuments from destruction by invading armies.

One of the earliest fortress-town was built in Jaisalmer in Thar Desert in 1156, a hub of caravan routes between Egypt, Arabia, Persia and India. The fort and all the houses were built with yellow ferruginous sandstone which takes a golden hue with the rising and setting sun (Fig. 39). The fort (Figs. 40-41) as well as the buildings within and outside the fort show intricate carvings (Fig. 42) and symbols which could be interpreted as both Hindu design with overtones of intercultural designs (Fig. 43). The stones of the walled city has been witness to life from the time of its construction to the present day where elderly Rajasthani's can be seen enjoying the warmth of the sandstone rocks heated by the desert's winter sun (Fig. 44). Not far from the fort is the mausoleum for departed souls of the nobles (Fig. 45) where the stones (Fig. 46) stand witness to a tradition not accepted by the society today. The Rajput princess along with her companions threw themselves into the funeral pyre of her husband killed in a battle for avoiding being violated by the victorious enemies. (Fig. 47)

Fig. 39: Jaisalmer – The rays of the sun caressing the stones

Fig. 40: Jaisalmer – I resisted like the Rajputs

Fig. 41: Jaisalmer – I will protect you from the invaders

Fig. 42: Jaisalmer – Image from yesterday and today

Fig. 43: Jaisalmer – Defying gravity

Fig. 44: Jaisalmer – A window of our history

Fig. 45: Jaisalmer – The warmth of the stones encourages dialogues

Fig. 46: Jaisalmer – It is here that our souls reside

Fig. 47: Jaisalmer – Sad witness to life terminated by immolation

UDAIPUR

The Rajput kings were open to other cultures as evident from the City Palace in Udaipur built by Maharana Udai Singh in the 16th century. Made of marble and semi-precious stones, a courtyard (Figs. 48-49) shows a blend of medieval European architecture and an intricate inlay work. The carvings on the Hindu temples in Udaipur show the same cultural tendency present in earlier temples (for instance Konarak) of mixing realty with the mythical with the ever present elephant (Fig. 50). Although the symbolism of cow and India has taken an enormous place in the eyes of the western world, the earlier paintings and carvings show that the rightful place should belong to the elephants. It is interesting to note that one of the most revered deity is Ganesh who bears the head of an elephant and not a cow.

Fig. 48: Udaipur – A romantic balcony

Fig. 49: Udaipur – Murmur of semi precious stones

Fig. 50: Udaipur – The elephants trumpet (I am an elephant as sacred as the cow)

SOUTH INDIA

South India treasures most of the Hindu temple architecture again using local stones with intricate, dense and detailed carvings that are not prevalent in the monuments in the North especially the Muslim architecture. One can imagine the time and devotion required to erect such monuments carved out of stones. (Fig. 51)

Fig. 51: South India – Patience and devotion

MODERN DAY MONUMENTS

The use of stone to embellish one's culture did not stop with the past history of India. The British invasion brought with it its own architecture and styling seen in many parts of India. However, the grandeur of the Indo-Islamic monuments has been evoked in the modern day monuments like the Bahai Temple, the Krishna Temple in New Delhi as well as mosques in South India

BAHAI TEMPLE

The stones remain a medium to represent our cultural heritages as seen by the Bahai temple (Fig. 52) erected in Delhi in the 20th century made out of marble and the form of lotus symbolizing peace and harmony, a cultural heritage dating back from centuries.

Fig. 52: Temple Bahai – The softness of the stones

KRISHNA TEMPLE of New Delhi

Fig. 53: Krishna Temple – Modern day devotion

MOSQUE of Kerala

Fig. 54: Mosque – Be pure as the marble

LOOKING BACK

Looking at the carved marble window of a Palace in Udaipur (Fig. 55) one tries to imagine the stories it can tell of the people who have peeped through, trying to discover and understand the cultural diversity of India.

Fig. 55: Looking back – Looking at the past

Index

C

D

E

F

S

T

U

V

❐ ❐ ❐